Radical Sports

KARTING

Graham Smith

H www.heinemann/library.co.uk
Visit our website to find out more information about Heinemann Library books.

To order:
☎ Phone 44 (0) 1865 888066
🖹 Send a fax to 44 (0) 1865 314091
💻 Visit the Heinemann Library Bookshop at www.heinemann/library.co.uk to browse our catalogue and order online.

First published in Great Britain by Heinemann Library,
Halley Court, Jordan Hill, Oxford OX2 8EJ,
a division of Reed Educational and Professional Publishing Ltd.
Heinemann is a registered trademark of Reed Educational & Professional Publishing Limited.

OXFORD   MELBOURNE   AUCKLAND
JOHANNESBURG   BLANTYRE   GABORONE
IBADAN   PORTSMOUTH NH (USA)   CHICAGO

© Reed Educational and Professional Publishing Ltd 2003
The moral right of the proprietor has been asserted.

Designed by Celia Floyd
Illustrations by Barry Atkinson
Originated by Universal
Printed in Hong Kong by Wing King Tong

ISBN 0 431 03692 6 (hardback)   ISBN 0 431 03700 0 (paperback)
07 06 05 04 03 02   07 06 05 04 03
10 9 8 7 6 5 4 3 2 1   10 9 8 7 6 5 4 3 2 1

British Library Cataloguing in Publication Data

Smith, Graham
   Karting. – (Radical sports)
   1. Karting – Juvenile literature
   1. Title
   796.7'6

Acknowledgements

The Publishers would like to thank the following for permission to reproduce photographs: Empics: 29; Malcolm Buckler: 4; PA Photos: 28, 29a; Chris Walker: 5, 6, 7, 8, 9a, 13a, 13c, 14, 17d, 19a, 19c, 19d, 20, 21, 22, 25, 26, 27; Graham Smith: 9b, 9c, 10, 11a, 11b, 11c, 12a, 12b, 13b, 15, 16, 17a, 17b, 17c, 19b, 24.

Cover photograph reproduced with permission of Chris Walker.

Our thanks to Peter Virgo and Jane Bingham for their help in the preparation of this book.

Every effort has been made to contact copyright holders of any material reproduced in this book. Any omissions will be rectified in subsequent printings if notice is given to the Publisher.

This book aims to cover all the essential techniques of this radical sport but it is important when learning a new sport to get expert tuition and to follow any manufacturers' instructions.

CONTENTS

INTRODUCTION

A short history of karting

The first kart was invented in 1956 by Art Ingels, an employee of a US racing-car company. The kart's **engine** came out of a lawnmower. When Ingels demonstrated the kart, another American, called Duffy Livingstone, saw it and decided to build his own. Soon the first race meetings were being held in the Rose Bowl car park in Pasadena, California.

In 1957, the first proper rule book was drawn up by the International Karting Federation, based in California. After this, karting spread rapidly across the USA. American airmen brought the sport to the UK and by 1962 there were karting **clubs** all over the world.

A very early kart race.

Changes in karting

Karts became more powerful and safer, with proper **brakes** instead of just a lever pressed against the rear tyre as in the original kart. Engines were also made especially for kart racing. The different types of karts were grouped into classes, for juniors and adults, and for the slower and faster types. Each class then had its own race at a meeting. Instead of straw bales lining the track, proper miniature racing circuits were made with permanent barriers.

The start of a Junior race.

Why go karting?

You can start racing from eight years old in most countries. Driving a kart is very exciting. But you need to learn how to control the kart first. As long as you practise the skills that are taught at all good kart schools you can make good progress and have great fun. Nearly every driver in Formula 1 started their racing life in karts.

Time for some advice before the start of a race.

WHAT IS A KART?

Racing karts are small, quick and great fun to drive. All the parts are mounted on a **frame** or **chassis**, made from steel tubing. The chassis twists to allow a smoother ride over bumps on the track. The kart shown opposite is a very popular type of kart for a beginner. It has a small **engine** that can be started by pulling on a cord. A racing kart like this will be able to reach speeds of up to 50 mph.

Wheels and tyres

The tyres are tubeless and filled with air. For dry weather, tyres are slick – meaning smooth with no tread – for maximum grip, as shown on the kart opposite. For wet weather, the tyres have to be changed to ones with treads, as shown here. The tread cuts through the water on the track. Slick tyres would slide too much in the wet.

Carburettor

This is the part of the engine that mixes the fuel with air to make an explosive mixture to be burnt inside the engine.

Rear bumper

This protects the back of the kart.

Brake disc

When the brake pedal is pushed two pads press against this disc to slow the kart down.

Rear axle

The rear wheels attach to the axle.

Bodywork side panels

These protect the driver and stop wheels from another kart interlocking and causing an accident.

Engine

This makes the kart move.

Fuel tank

This holds the fuel for the engine.

Seat

The driver has to be a tight fit in the seat. This is so you do not bounce about and so you can keep good control of the kart.

Front bumper and nose cone

These protect the driver's feet.

Accelerator pedal

A cable connects the pedal to the **carburettor**. Pressing down the pedal lets more fuel mixture into the engine so that the kart can go faster.

Brake pedal

This is connected to a **brake** to slow the kart down. When you push your left foot down on the brake pedal, two pads push against the brake disc attached to the rear axle.

Chassis

The chassis is made of steel tubing that is flexible enough to twist a little as it goes around corners. Most of the parts of the kart are bolted onto the frame.

Steering wheel

The steering is very direct – less than half a turn on the steering wheel makes the kart do a full turn.

CLOTHES AND EQUIPMENT

Since a kart can go quite fast, it is very important to wear equipment that protects your hands, head and body, but most of all your head, just in case you should fall out. The first few times you go karting you should rent all the equipment you need. If you decide to go karting regularly you will probably want to buy your own. Buy approved equipment from a specialist karting shop.

Helmet

The helmet must have a safety label to show that it is approved. It is very important to buy a helmet that fits reasonably tightly so that it cannot be pushed off when fastened. Buy the best helmet you can to protect your head. The helmet also has a visor to protect your eyes from flying stones and other debris.

Racesuit

The racesuit is designed to protect your body if you should come out of the kart in an accident. Even if you skid along the ground, it will not wear through. You must wear a racesuit that is approved as safe to use. Colour choice is up to you, some manufacturers will let you design your own.

Gloves

Any strong gloves without holes, usually leather or leather substitutes. You can buy proper racing gloves with padding to stop blisters and a Velcro fastener to prevent the gloves sliding off your hands.

Boots

They must cover and protect your ankles from knocks. High top trainers can be worn but most people buy proper racing boots. They will have a thinner sole for a better feel of the pedals.

Earplugs

It is advisable to wear earplugs when you are out on your kart, to protect your hearing against excessive noise. Buy them at the specialist kart shop or a hardware store.

Rain suit

If it is wet you can buy a one-piece rain suit – commonly called a 'wet suit'. You wear the rain suit over your racesuit to keep it dry.

Safety label

Make sure that the equipment you buy has a safety label like this one, to show that it is approved.

A KART OF YOUR OWN

Once you have learnt the basic karting skills, you may decide that you would like to have a kart of your own. If you don't want your own, some kart schools and racing teams will hire out everything you need to go racing.

There is a very wide range of karts, so it is important to make the right choice. Go to your local outdoor track and see what other people of your age are racing. Look at adverts in karting magazines, or at your local **club**. You will need the help of an expert adult in choosing a kart. Sometimes a second-hand sale will include a kart stand and wet weather wheels and tyres – all items you will need to go racing. You will also need some basic tools. Some karts will fit in the back of a car, but if not, an alternative is to tow a small trailer for the kart.

Engines

There are different classes of karts, grouped by **engine** size and type. Engine size is measured in cc (cubic centimetres) and engines can be either 2-stroke or 4-stroke. The 2-stroke engines need to have oil mixed into the fuel. They are lighter and give more power for their size. The most popular sizes of 2-stroke engines are 100cc and 125cc. The 4-stroke engines are cheaper to buy and run, but are a little larger and therefore heavier. They need fuel straight from the pump.

Cadet ············➤

60cc, 2-stroke, with an extra small kart **chassis** for 8- to 12-year-olds. Easy to drive, with speeds up to 55 mph.

Junior 2-stroke ·········►

A very popular starting point for drivers aged 11 years and above. Slightly more powerful than the Junior 4-stroke with speeds up to 65 mph.

········ Junior Gearbox

85cc, 2-stroke engine with six **gears**, like a bicycle with gears. Age ranges vary from country to country, but will cater for 13 years upwards. Speeds up to 70 mph.

◄······ Junior Intercontinental A

A 100cc, 2-stroke class for championships. Not recommended for beginners. Speeds up to 70 mph.

Junior 4-stroke

(see the kart on page 7)
A single- or twin-engined kart with 4-stroke industrial engines, often from Honda or Briggs and Stratton. A good economical starting point for beginners, if your local club offers the class. For 11 years upwards. Speeds up to 60 mph.

SAFETY FIRST

Make sure you fit in the kart properly. You should be able to press the pedals right down without fully straightening your legs. You should be able to reach the top of the steering wheel while still keeping your back firmly against the seat.

KEEPING FIT

You might think keeping fit is not important because you are simply sitting down in your kart. You would be wrong. A strong upper body and general over-all fitness is extremely important because you will be working hard at steering, braking and keeping yourself in the seat going round corners. For general fitness concentrate on activities like skipping, jogging, cycling or swimming. Press-ups are very good for strengthening your arms and upper body.

Warm-up

Before you go out to race, you should warm-up to get your body properly prepared, perhaps by skipping or running on the spot. Then it's a good idea to perform some stretching exercises as these can prevent injuries. The examples given are just some of those you can do.

Skipping can be a useful warm-up exercise.

Hamstring stretch

Bend one knee while keeping the other leg out straight with your heel on the floor. You will feel the muscles in your calf and behind your knee stretch. Repeat with the opposite leg.

Quadricep stretch ···▶

Stand with your feet flat on the floor, knees together. Lift
one foot up behind you and use one hand to pull it in
towards your bottom. Gently tilt hips forward. You will feel
a stretch in the front of your bent thigh.

Upper back stretch ······················▶

Soften your knees. Clasp your hands and
push forwards. You will feel a stretch across
your upper back.

Cool-down

While driving, you will have been in a
fairly fixed position so you might be a
little stiff. So, when you come in off the
track, do the stretch exercises again.

The right food

Fruit and pasta dishes are the right
kinds of food to eat before karting
because they are light, yet give you
energy. Don't eat in the hour before
going out on the track. Drink plenty
of liquids but not anything containing
caffeine or too much sugar. They may
give you a quick boost but it will not last.

Bring some of your own food with you to the race
weekends, as you cannot guarantee to be able to buy
the right sort of food at the track.

SAFETY FIRST

🏁   Try to drink a bottle of water for
    every race, more in hot weather.

YOUR FIRST TIME ON A RACE KART

Many people's first experience of karting is at an 'arrive and drive' karting track where you can begin driving with very little proper instruction. However, the best way to start is at an approved kart school. Contact your national karting organization or local club for a list of schools.

Before you start driving you must learn the basic flag signals. The track marshals use different coloured flags to give messages to the drivers.

The black flag is to tell you to come in to the pits, perhaps because you have made a mistake and they want to talk to you.

The chequered flag means it is the end of the session, so come in to the pits. When you slow down to come in, raise one arm in the air so everyone can see you are slowing.

The yellow flag means there is an accident ahead, so slow down and do not overtake anyone.

In the kart

The instructor will make sure you fit properly in the kart and can easily reach the pedals and the steering wheel. Get the instructor to push the kart along so you can try the brake before the **engine** is started.

Most likely you will walk around the track before you go out in the kart, so that you can learn the layout. Alternatively the instructor may use a map of the track.

The instructor will start the engine for you. Put your foot on the brake while the engine is being started. Find out how you switch it off.

When the engine is running and you push the right-hand accelerator pedal, it makes the kart start moving and go faster. Never press both pedals at the same time. Apply the brakes gently at first, but enough to slow the kart down. Take your foot off the brake before turning into the corners and do not rest your foot on the pedal because it can make the brake too hot.

Look for a clear gap between other karts before you join the track. Take it steady to begin with.

Place your hands at a quarter to three or ten to two position on the steering wheel. Use one hand and arm to pull the steering wheel towards you to turn, while the other keeps the steering steady.

SAFETY FIRST

⚑ Remember to close the visor on your safety helmet before you go out, so that stones or debris cannot reach your eyes.

DRIVING SKILLS

The 'racing line'

Once you know how to control the kart, it is time to learn the correct and fastest way round the track. The quickest way is called the 'racing line'. Try to imagine this drawn on the track like the example in the picture, so that you can follow it.

3 Apex

Aim for the centre of the corner and the inside edge of the track. This is called the apex or clipping point.

4 Racing line

Then start accelerating and guide the kart so that it moves over to the left side of the track on the way out of the corner. Do not try and force the kart, it should flow naturally along the racing line.

2 Turn-in point

Come off the brake and turn the steering wheel when you reach the turn-in point. The turn-in point is where you start turning the steering wheel to guide the kart along the imaginary racing line round the corner.

1 Braking point

Approaching a corner, you first find the correct braking point. This is the point where you start pressing the **brake** pedal and can slow down enough to take the corner safely. For example, if the corner turns to the right, you will need to be as far over to the left as possible on the straight.

This driver is pulling the kart to the side of the track where it is safer.

Spinning

If you do spin round or go off the track and are able to restart, then look for a gap between approaching karts before carrying on. If you cannot restart, raise your arms. The instructor will tell you whether to stay in the kart until someone reaches you, or whether you should get out and run off the track to a safer place behind the barriers.

Getting your licence

When you have mastered all the driving skills, you will be ready to apply for a competition licence. To gain this, you will have to pass a two-part **ARKS test**. One part will be a written paper testing your knowledge of karting rules and regulations. The other part will be a driving test. If you do not pass first time, don't worry; you can re-take the test later. Listen carefully to the feedback from your test instructor.

TOP TIP

⚑ Find out about the entry and exit points on the circuit before you go out on your kart.

SAFETY FIRST

⚑ Check the brakes work properly before you go out. Push the kart along and press the brake to make it stop.

PRACTISING YOUR RACING SKILLS

Before you are allowed to practise, you must sign on and pay a fee. Your parent or guardian will be required to counter-sign against your name to show they have given permission.

Every time you go out on the track, build up speed gradually. When you first go out, the tyres will be cold and will not grip the track well. Once you have gone round the track once or twice, the tyres will heat up and give more grip, then you can go faster.

When you have mastered following the racing line round the track, try going faster. **Brake** a little later and a little harder at each corner. Find someone to time each of your laps with a stopwatch so you can find out how much you are improving. Do about eight laps at a time and then come in to find out how you are doing. The kart may need some adjustments to help you drive faster.

More flag signals

It is important to know all the different flag signals that you may come across while on a race track. The flag signals below, along with the ones shown on page 12, could all be seen while driving.

The red flag signifies the race or practice session is being temporarily halted, perhaps because of a serious incident. Slow down and be prepared to stop where the marshals indicate. Do not overtake anyone.

The black flag with an orange disc means you have a mechanical fault and should call in to the pits.

The blue flag means someone is close behind or trying to overtake.

The white flag means there is a slow moving vehicle on the track.

The black and white diagonal flag is for giving warnings about poor behaviour to drivers.

SAFETY FIRST

Learn all the flag signals to ensure you will know how to behave safely on the circuit.

RACE PREPARATION

Entries

Join the kart **club** where you plan to race most often. They will supply you with entry forms for their races. Send your entry off with the fee at least two weeks before the race. Remember to show you are a novice on the form. Your parent or guardian will have to sign too.

Number plates and numbers

Different classes often have different coloured number plates. It is usual for novice drivers to have black number plates with white numbers. When you enter a race, you need to pick a number between 16 and 99. If someone else has picked the same number the club officials will give you a different number when you arrive. The low numbers are reserved for the top national championship drivers.

The kart tracks

Kart tracks are usually about 1000 metres long but older drivers can race on the longer motor racing circuits. **Sprint** races last about ten minutes while **endurance** races last several hours.

Class weights

Each class has a minimum weight limit so that lighter drivers don't have too much of an advantage. This minimum weight includes the kart and the driver with all his or her gear. If the kart does not reach the minimum weight, blocks of lead ballast are fixed on to make up the weight.

The driver and kart are weighed after a race so there is less chance of anyone cheating by removing weight before the race.

The officials

The Clerk of the Course is the boss – he or she runs the race meeting and makes all the important decisions. If you do anything against the rules, the Clerk of the Course will want to see you for an interview. The Steward makes sure the meeting is organized as per the rules and will also sign your **licence** if you finish your races. The Secretary of the Meeting does all the paperwork and receives the entries. The Chief **Scrutineer** and his staff make sure your kart meets all the technical regulations. The Marshals are the track workers who wave the flags and keep the track clear.

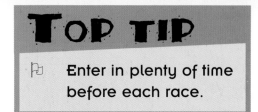

TOP TIP

⚑ Enter in plenty of time before each race.

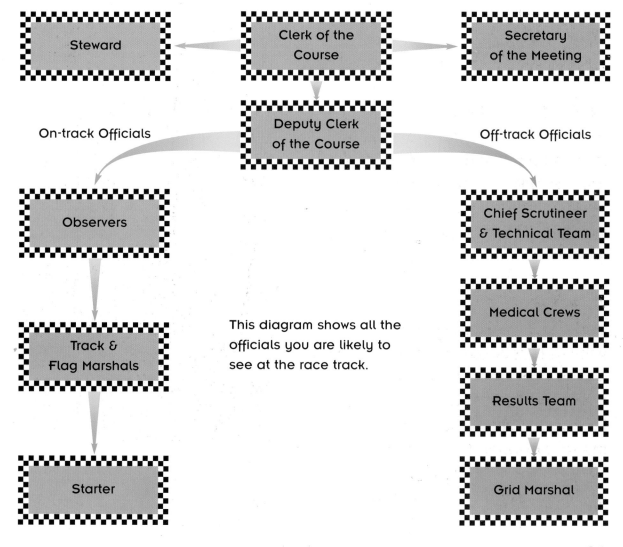

This diagram shows all the officials you are likely to see at the race track.

YOUR FIRST RACE

Arrive early at the track so that, if allowed, you can walk round and set up before it all starts. Ask permission from an official first and make sure you are back well before the time for starting. Find out where the start and finish lines are, if you don't already know.

Signing on and scrutineering

Take your competition **licence** to race control and sign on for the meeting. You should receive a **scrutineering** card to complete with your kart and **engine** details. Take this, your kart, and all your **racewear** to the scrutineering area to have it all checked by officials. Leave your licence with the organizers to have it signed to show you have safely finished your races.

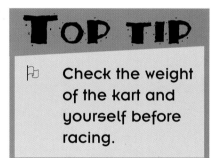

TOP TIP

Check the weight of the kart and yourself before racing.

Drivers briefing and official practice

All drivers must attend the briefing given by the Clerk of the Course. He or she will explain anything special that happens at the track – for example, where to stop if the race is halted. Immediately after this, there will be a short official practice session. It is important to be seen to do at least three laps in this session.

The start of a race.

Heats

Unless there is timed qualifying, each driver will have two or three heats, with novices starting at the back. Make sure you find out your starting position. Your combined

TOP TIP

⚐ Don't leave home without your licence and remember to pick it up after the race.

results from the heats will determine your starting position for the finals. Make sure you and your kart are on the **grid** in plenty of time for each race. The starting positions are usually marked out with 1 and 2 at the front and the higher numbers at the back.

Finals

If there are more drivers in the class than the maximum for a race, there could be a B or even a C Final. The first four in these races win a place at the back of the grid for the next final. The B Final, sometimes called a *repêchage*, is the last chance to get into the A Final. The trophies are given to the winners and top places from the A Final. After each race, you might be called in for technical checks or to be weighed. Do not leave the area until given permission.

Prize giving

This usually takes place after all the races are complete. Even if you have not won a trophy, it is polite to stay and applaud those who have and some clubs have trophies for the best novice. Someday you will be winning trophies and will be looking for an appreciative audience.

A driver receiving his trophy.

TAKING CARE OF YOUR KART

Karts may look quite simple, but there are many adjustments possible to make them go better at each track you visit. Always have an expert adult check any work you do yourself. Until you are experienced, adults should carry out the adjustments.

Gear ratios and sprockets

The **engine** is connected to the rear **axle sprocket** with a chain to make the rear wheels turn round, just like on a bicycle. Many karts have an automatic **clutch**. This allows the engine to be started and tick over without moving the kart. When you press the accelerator pedal the clutch makes the engine drive the chain. The large sprocket fixed to the rear axle needs to be changed for the different speeds found at different tracks. A smaller sprocket will give the kart a higher top speed. Oil the chain with chain-spray before every outing.

Ensure that the gear sprocket is oiled regularly.

Fuel

The engine burns petrol to make it go. Always have an adult mix the fuel and fill the fuel tank.

Tyres

The tyres need to be filled with air using a foot pump or compressor. The amount of air in the tyre is called the tyre pressure. You can check the pressure with a tyre pressure gauge. The higher the pressure, the faster the tyre will warm up so, to start with while you are learning, you might try slightly higher pressures than you would for a race.

Setting up the handling

The handling of your kart is the way that it feels to drive. There are adjustments you can try. For example, moving the wheels in or out on the axles decides whether the back or front of the kart slides first going round a corner. Keep a book recording all your settings and times on each track.

Wet weather

Put on the wet weather treaded tyres in place of the slick tyres. Generally, set the front wheels further apart and the rear wheels closer together than for the dry weather.

TOP TIP

- Keep your kart clean at all times. When you clean it, you will notice any loose nuts and bolts.

TOOLS

You will need various tools to look after your kart:

- Tyre pressure gauge and foot pump
- Set of Allen keys
- Spanners
- T-bars to fit wheel nuts
- Spark plug spanner
- Pliers, side-cutters, screwdrivers
- **Chain-splitter**
- Stopwatch
- Fire extinguisher

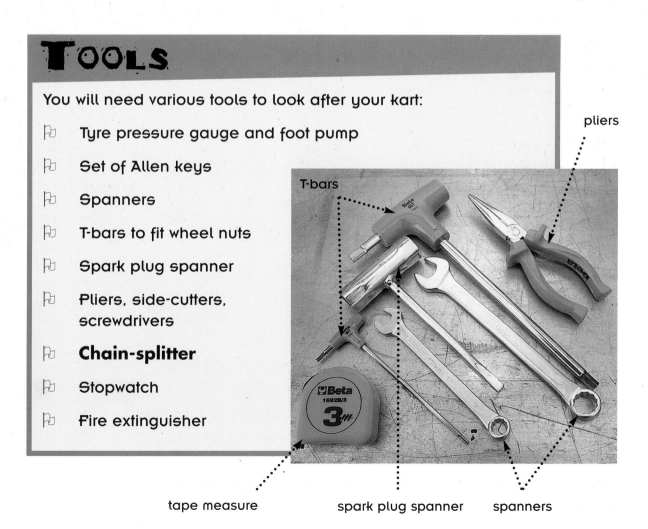

pliers

T-bars

tape measure

spark plug spanner

spanners

TAKING IT FURTHER

To begin with, you will race in your local club championship, getting points for each race you complete. Then you will want to race at other clubs and learn other tracks. After that, you may enter the national championships. Karting is a worldwide sport. The CIK, the world governing body for karting, organizes continental and world championships.

This is a national race.

UK championships

In the UK, the Super 1 Series organizes the British Championships for **direct-drive** seniors and juniors, the Champions of the Future series organizes the Cadet British Championship, and the British Superkart Association organizes the British Championship for the 250cc **gearbox** class. The winner of a top championship can use the number 1 on his or her kart for the next year and the top places also have the right to use the number showing their finishing position.
These are the 'cherished numbers' for 'seeded drivers'.

European championships

Drivers come from all over the world to compete in the European championships. There are classes for Formula A, Intercontinental A, Junior Intercontinental A and ICC (the 125cc gearbox class). Only the best at each round will reach the finals. The top drivers in these series will often progress to become household names in Formula 1 motor racing.

Racing in the USA

The biggest races in the USA are the Grand Nationals and the Super Nationals. There are about 550 tracks in the USA and Canada and 120,000 or so drivers. Most drivers compete in **sprint** races, with the rest doing **speedway** or **endurance** events.

World championships

The World CIK/FIA Championship is held for a limited number of professional teams, contesting races in North America, Europe and Japan in Formula Super A. These drivers can earn good salaries, driving for kart manufacturers. There are a couple of practice days, then timed qualifying, some heats and two points-scoring finals. This series is the Formula 1 of karting.

This race is part of an international competition.

RACING STARS

Lots of kart drivers race for many years and take immense enjoyment from participating in the sport. But many other drivers progress from karting to race full-sized cars and some become very famous. Below are some of the latest stars in motor racing who progressed from a karting background.

Jenson Button

Jenson started racing Cadet karts in 1989 and soon became virtually unbeatable in the category. He raced in the British Championships Super 1 Series and took the Junior British title. By the end of 1994, he was racing for top Italian teams, coming second in the World Formula A in 1995. Then he was a full professional kart driver for two more years, racing all over the world. He made the move into single-seater race cars in 1998, winning the Formula Ford Festival and moving straight on to Formula 3. His third place in a relatively uncompetitive car, and in his rookie year, led to a Formula 1 test and a drive in the Williams Grand Prix car for 2000. Then in 2001 he moved to the Renault Formula 1 Grand Prix team.

Memo Gidley

Mexican-born Memo was raised in San Rafael, California and started out racing sailboats, BMX bikes and motocross. In order to pursue his dream of becoming a racing driver, he enrolled in a race mechanics course and, in exchange for working on the cars, he was allowed to race. He was so good that a kart team signed him up. He won many races in 100 cc and in **gearbox** karts, then started to race cars again as well. In 1995 he became the Oval Course Champion in US Formula Ford

2000. He progressed up the single-seater ladder until, in 1999, he raced for the first time in the top US Champcars series – the series that is making him a household name in the USA. He continues to race karts regularly and holds racing workshops for youngsters.

Mark Webber

Australian Mark started karting in 1991 and the following year won the New South Wales and ACT Karting Championship. By 1994 he was racing Formula Ford, both in Australia and later in the UK. Then he went on to race in the British Formula 3 single-seater series, where he gained fourth place in 1997 and came to the attention of the top AMG Mercedes team. For the next couple of years he raced the fabulous CLK Mercedes GT cars, before returning to single seaters in Formula 3000 – one step below Formula 1. Now he has been signed to drive Formula 1 cars.

GLOSSARY

ARKS Test the UK's Novice Driver Test that must be completed and passed satisfactorily before a competition licence is issued

axle a rod on which wheels are mounted

brake slows or stops the kart

carburettor the part, fitted to the engine, that takes in the fuel (petrol) and air to mix before it enters the engine

chain-splitter a tool that separates a chain, so that links may be removed or added, to change the length of the chain

chassis (see frame)

club the body that organizes a kart race – you must be a member of a kart club to race

clutch the mechanism that disconnects the engine from driving the kart

direct-drive kart the class of kart where the engine is directly connected to the sprocket on the rear axle by a chain or belt

endurance long distance races held over several hours using a team of drivers for each kart

engine the unit that provides the power to make the kart move; it may be 2-stroke or 4-stroke

frame steel tubes that are welded together to carry axles, engine, seat and all other parts of the kart

gearbox kart a kart equipped with several gears that can be changed at will by the driver

gears a mechanism of cogged wheels that change the engine speed

grid the predetermined order for starting a race – the dummy grid is the area where karts park in that order before moving out onto the track for the actual race

licence a certificate of registration issued by the organizing body; the holder is presumed to know and abide by the rules

long-circuit sprint racing on the long, full-size motor-racing tracks

pits the part of the circuit where karts may come off the track to refuel or make repairs; also known as the paddock

racewear the approved safety clothing worn when riding the kart

scrutineering the technical check to ensure the kart is safe to race, and complies with the regulations

speedway races on short, oval dirt tracks

sprint the most popular form of racing having two or three heats and a final

sprocket a round plate with teeth to fit into the chain links

USEFUL ADDRESSES

Motor Sports Association
Motor Sports House
Riverside Park
Colnbrook
Slough
SL3 0HG
Tel: 01753 765000
This is the governing body for the UK.

Association of British Kart Clubs
    There are about forty clubs in the UK
    and most are members of the ABkC.
Association of Racing Kart Schools
    They can supply a list of approved kart
    schools.
Both at: Stoneycroft
        Godsons Lane
        Napton
        Southam
        CV47 8LX

Australia

Australian Karting Association (AKA)
PO Box S104
St. Clair
NSW 2759
Tel: 2 9623 4351
(Each state has an office of the AKA)

FURTHER READING

Books

How to Start Kart Racing, Graham Smith, TFM
Publishing Ltd

Magazines

Karting Magazine, Lodgemark Press, 15,
Moorfield Road, Orpington, Kent, BR6 0XD
Tel: 01689 897123

Kart Oz, PO Box 2154, Fountain Gate,
Victoria 3805, Australia

All the Internet addresses (URLs) given in this book
were valid at the time of going to press. However,
due to the dynamic nature of the Internet, some
addresses may have changed, or sites may have
ceased to exist since publication. While the author
and publishers regret any inconvenience this may
cause readers, no responsibility for any such
changes can be accepted by either the author or
the publishers.

Websites

UK

www.abkc.org.uk
Association of British Kart Clubs

www.arks.co.uk
Association of Racing Kart Schools

www.msauk.org
Motor Sports Association

www.karting.co.uk
UK Karting

World

www.fia.com
International Automobile Federation

Australia

www.aka.asn.au
Australian Karting Association (AKA)

www.nkn.com.au
National Karting News

INDEX